Simple Experiments in Time

with Everyday Materials

Muriel Mandell

Illustrated by Frances Zweifel

Sterling Publishing Co., Inc.   New York

*In memory of lifelong collaborator Horace Mandell
and for Aviva Michaela Mandell, the future*

Library of Congress Cataloging-in-Publication Data

Mandell, Muriel.
    Simple experiments in time with everyday materials / Muriel
Mandell ; illustrated by Frances Zweifel.
        p.   cm.
    Includes index.
    ISBN 0-8069-3803-X
    1. Time measurements—Experiments. I. Zweifel, Frances
W. II. Title.
QB213.M36   1997
529.7'078—dc21   97–992
                                                                    CIP
                                                                    AC

10 9 8 7 6 5 4 3 2 1

Published by Sterling Publishing Company, Inc.
387 Park Avenue South, New York, N.Y. 10016
© 1997 by Muriel Mandell
Distributed in Canada by Sterling Publishing
c/o Canadian Manda Group, One Atlantic Avenue, Suite 105
Toronto, Ontario, Canada M6K 3E7
Distributed in Australia by Capricorn Link (Australia) Pty Ltd.
P.O. Box 6651, Baulkham Hills, Business Centre, NSW 2153, Australia
Manufactured in the United States of America
All rights reserved

Sterling ISBN 0-8069-3803-X

CONTENTS

1. TALKING ABOUT TIME

We use the word "time" to refer to *when* something happens (date) or *how long* an event lasts (interval).

People have measured time by the Sun, Moon, and stars, by the use of oil and candles and by water and sand, with weights and pendulums, with batteries and electric power stations, and in this century with the atoms of a metal called *cesium*.

In prehistoric times, people needed to know only the seasons and night and day. Now physicists, studying particles of the atom, measure a picosecond, a trillionth of a second. And other scientists—paleontologists, geologists, archeologists, biologists—use "radioactive clocks" and "molecular clocks" to measure billions of years.

Astronomers, physicists, engineers, statisticians—as well as blacksmiths and locksmiths—were all involved in the development of the measuring stick for time, "the clock." Horologists (clock-makers) based their inventions on the scientific theories of Newton, Descartes, Galileo, Niels Bohr, and Einstein, among others.

But it was natural phenomena—the spinning of the Earth on its axis and the rotation of the Earth around the Sun—that provided the first means of measuring time.

Now and Then

We use words about time all the time. You can play a game with a friend—or even challenge yourself—to see how many you can jot down in ten or fifteen minutes.

You need:
a timer or a clock
pencil and paper

What to do:
Set a kitchen timer or a clock with an alarm before you sit down with pencil and paper. Then list as many words and expressions about time as you can think of before the alarm goes off. "Then" and "before" are both examples—and so are expressions such as "in time" and "split second."

What happens:
You can check our list on page 9. Did you miss any? Did we miss any of yours?

TIME TO WAKE UP

Scientists have discovered that the two sides of our brain do different things. The left brain has a strong sense of time; the right has none. But when we tell ourselves to wake up at a particular time, the right brain is the one that understands and wakes us. See whether the two sides of your brain cooperate. Try waking at a particular time without an alarm clock—or someone helping you.

How Long Is a Minute?

Do you know exactly how much time it takes before a minute has gone by? Have fun with your friends by seeing who can come closest to "timing" a minute!

You need:

a watch with a second hand

one or more friends

pencil and paper

What to do:

Take turns. A friend holds the watch and gives a signal. You then put your hands on your lips and keep quiet until you think one minute is up—and then shout "Time!" Your friend will record your time. Then you take over the timing while your friend keeps quiet for what *seems* like a minute and you record the time.

Compare times.

What happens:

You will find that a minute can be quite a long time!

Why:

Time drags when you're concentrating on time passing. But try timing a minute when you are reading or drawing or playing a game and see how short a minute can seem.

The Time of Your Life

A "timeline" is a list of the dates of significant events in the order in which they occurred. You can make a timeline of your life, giving the dates of the important things that have happened to you.

You need:
pencil and paper

What to do:
Sit down and think about things that have mattered to you. Perhaps talk to your parents about dates that you aren't sure of. Make a list of all the things that occur to you—your birth date, when you first walked and talked, the time you entered kindergarten, when you learned to read, trips you went on, the date you first learned to ride a bike or to skate, the arrival of a sister or brother, a prize you won, a play you were in, when you met your best friend, your graduation from school.

Order them according to date and then make a timeline such as the one on page 11. Liven it up with drawings if you wish. Later, you may want to revise your timeline because other things have become more important. And you may find it interesting to consult with your parents and your grandparents and make timelines of the events in their lives.

Hatched -------- May 17
Caught lizard ------ July 5
Escaped coyote --- July 6
1st Nest ---

8

Time Words and Expressions

(Answer to "Now and Then" on page 6)

after
after a while
afternoon
all the time
already
any time
as soon as
at once
before
biennial
bimonthly
biweekly
century
chronology
circadian
concurrent
contemporary
constant
continual
continuous
daily
day
double time
diurnal
during
earlier
early
eon
epoch
equinox
evening
era
eternal

eventually
final
first
for a second,
  a minute, an
  hour, a month,
  a season, a
  year
for a while
forever
fortnight
frequent
future
hitherto
horology
hour
immediate
in a flash
in a minute
infinite
infrequent
instantly
intermittent
interval
last month,
  week, year
late
later
latest
long ago
meanwhile
midnight
millennium

minute
momentary
month
morning
nanosecond
never
next month,
  week, year
night
nocturnal
noon
now
now and then
o'clock
on time
once in a while
once upon a
  time
overtime
past
picosecond
perpetual
present
previously
quicker
quickest
quickly
rapidly
seasonal
second
sequence
sequential
slower

slowest
slowly
sometimes
split second
sudden
synchronize
tempo
temporal
temporary
then
this month,
  week, year
timeless
timely
today
tomorrow
tonight
ultimate
ultrashort
vernal
week
when
while
year
yearlong
year-round
yesterday
yesteryear
yet
Yule
zero hour

2. TELLING TIME BY THE MOON

Some scientists—called archeoastronomists—combine the study of the stars and planets with the study of ancient civilizations. These scientists have studied 10,000-year-old bones found in Africa and Europe. They think grooves carved into them may be primitive calendars used to follow the cycles of the Moon throughout the year.

Before our early ancestors became concerned with the hour of the day, they were involved with day and night, with the month and the seasons of the year. Peoples of many different cultures observed the phases of the Moon and the movements of the Sun and stars. They used them to keep time, so they would know when to plant and when to harvest.

The pyramids in Egypt and the Yucatan, as well as rock foundations such as England's Stonehenge, all indicated those important times of the year and the religious holidays that celebrated those times and pacified their gods.

CALENDAR TIMELINE

4242 BC	Egyptian lunar calendar
3761 BC	Jewish lunar calendar
3300 BC	Possible date of first Mayan calendar
3100 BC	Egyptian solar calendar
3000 BC	Mesopotamian and Athenian lunar calendars
2680 BC	Egypt's Great Pyramids built
2637 BC	Chinese calendar invented by legendary Emperor Huangdi
1600 BC	England's Stonehenge erected
753 BC	Founding of Rome
600 BC	Zoroastrian calendar with year starting at vernal equinox—still used in Islamic Iran
46 BC	Julius Caesar revises Roman calendar
500	Dionysius Exiguus proposes using the term Anno Domini (AD), the Year of Our Lord
622	Hijri calendar
900's	Mayan calendar more exact than modern calendar
1077	Jalali calendar devised by Omar Khayyam of Persia
1100	Mayan pyramid in Yucatan
1582	Gregorian calendar
1752	Great Britain and colonies abandon Julian calendar.
1844	Badi' calendar of the Baha'i Faith
1873	Buddhists in Japan adopt Gregorian calendar
1917	USSR adopts Gregorian calendar
1957	India adopts Gregorian calendar

About Calendars

Calendars are orderly plans that fit days into months and months into years.

As far back as 3000 BC, Babylonians—who lived in what is now part of Iraq—and Egyptians devised lunar calendars. They were made up of 354 days with months based on the cycles of the Moon. The Athenians had a similar calendar.

Later, because the life-saving floods came every 365 days, the Egyptians changed to a solar year, with a calendar of 12 months, each with 30 days. This left five extra days at the end of the year during which the people celebrated the birthdays of important gods.

The Romans originally had a lunar year of 355 days, but by the time of Julius Caesar, the Roman calendar was three months ahead of the Sun's year. In 45 BC, Caesar reformed the calendar, bringing it closer to the one we use today. He added almost three months to the year 46 BC and, like the Egyptians, devised a solar calendar of 365 days. He added an extra day every fourth year, our Leap Year. This calendar, called the Julian calendar, was used throughout the Middle Ages.

It wasn't until 500 years after his death that time was related to the birth of Christ. Many non-Christian societies use CE (Common Era) instead of AD (Anno Domini, the Year of Our Lord) and BCE (Before the Common Era) instead of BC (before Christ). The Muslim Hijri calendar starts counting from AH (Anno Hegirae), the Year of the Emigration—the journey of Mohammed from Mecca to Medina.

Because the year was still too long by about 11 minutes, the Julian calendar was more than a week off by the 16th century. Eventually, Easter would coincide with the previous Christmas! So, in 1582 Pope Gregory XIII wiped out 10 days (October 5 became October 15), and decreed that no century year, such as 1700, should be a leap year unless it was divisible by 400. That meant that three leap years would be omitted every four centuries. Also, the calendar year was to begin on January 1 instead of March 21. September through December were to keep their original names—meaning the 7th, 8th, 9th, and 10th months of the year—even though they were now the 9th to 12th months of a year that began in January. This Gregorian calendar is the one we use today.

The Chinese calendar, devised about 2700 BC, reckoned time with numbered months and years named for 12 different animals. It's still used for setting the dates of the festivals of the Harvest Moon and of the New Year (which is celebrated

between January 20th and February 19th on the Gregorian calendar).

The Orthodox Eastern Church still uses the Julian calendar, so Greek Catholics celebrate Christmas a number of days after other Christians.

Moon Time

To know when to plant their seeds, and to fix the dates of religious holidays, many ancient peoples devised calendars based on the Moon. One of the first words for Moon meant "the measure of time." The word *"month"* comes from the Moon—*moonth*. You can use a lamp and an ordinary ball to see what causes the various phases of the Moon.

You need:
electric lamp
a white tennis ball
pencil and paper

What to do:
Place the lighted lamp on a table in a darkened room. Hold the ball in your hand at arm's length with your back to the light. Raise the ball high enough to allow the light to strike the ball. Note the part of the ball lighted by the lamp. This represents the full moon. Turn around slowly from right to left keeping the ball in front of you and above your head. Observe the change in shape of the lighted part of the ball as you make one complete turn. Stop at each one-eighth turn and draw the shape of the ball (the Moon) that is lit up.

What happens:
You will observe the various phases of the Moon from the full moon to the half moon to a crescent sliver to the new moon when no part is lit.

Why:
Every day the Moon rises and sets about 50 minutes later than the day before, taking about four weeks to go around Earth. During that time the Moon waxes

from new moon to full moon and then wanes to new moon again. The same half of the Moon always faces Earth as the Moon goes around it. Half of the Moon is lighted by the Sun and half is in darkness. Actually you see a little more than half because Earth's gravity causes the Moon to librate—to vibrate—as it rotates. At new moon the half facing Earth is dark because the Moon is between Earth and the Sun. Of course, you often see the Moon in its various phases in the night sky. But you can also see the crescent moon and the half moon during the day because they rise before nightfall.

DIFFERENT DRUMMERS

Some societies set up their calendars to start with the year of their rulers, with the founding of a city, or with an important event in their religion. The Greeks measured time by referring to the Olympiads, the first of which was held in 776 BC.

Even now, the Hopi Indians express time in their language by what happens "when the corn matures" or "when a sheep grows up." The Trobriand Islanders, off New Guinea, date events by saying they occurred "during the childhood of X" or "in the year of the marriage of Y."

String Calendar

The string calendar comes from Sumatra, an Indonesian island in the Indian Ocean. You can make one for yourself by threading string through each of 30 holes in a sheet of heavy paper as a way of recording the passing of days in a lunar month. Pencil and paper or a bought calendar may be easier ways to keep track of the days of the month, but your own string calendar can amuse your friends.

You need:
sheet of heavy paper
paper punch or scissors
long piece of heavy thread or string

What to do:
Fold your paper lengthwise in half and then in half again. Punch 7 evenly spaced holes in each of the first three-quarters of the page. In 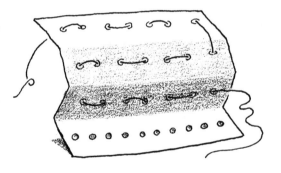 the last quarter punch 10 holes, as in the illustration. On the first of the month, knot your string and thread it through the first hole. The next day, thread the string through the second hole. Do the same every day of the month. When you want to know what day of the month it is, just count the number of holes you've covered.

Perpetual Calendar

You can find out the day of the week on which you were born. Indeed, you can find the day of the week of any date from 1920 to 2019.

You need:
the charts on pages 18–19
your birth date

What to do:
(1) First check the Years column for the letter next to the year of your birth. (2) Under Months look for your letter and find which number falls under the month in which you were born. (3) Under Days use the number you just found and go down to the date on which you were born

What happens:
For example, if you were born on July 19, 1986: (1) Your letter is B. (2) Your number is 1. (3) You were born on a Friday.

Amaze your friends and tell them the day of the week on which they were born. You can also find out about your parents or a historical figure, as long as you know their birth dates.

YEARS

1920 K	1940 H	1960 L	1980 I	2000 M
1921 F	1941 C	1961 G	1981 D	2001 A
1922 G	1942 D	1962 A	1982 E	2002 B
1923 A	1943 E	1963 B	1983 F	2003 C
1924 I	1944 M	1964 J	1984 N	2004 K
1925 D	1945 A	1965 E	1985 B	2005 F
1926 K	1946 B	1966 F	1986 C	2006 G
1927 F	1947 C	1967 G	1987 D	2007 A
1928 N	1948 K	1968 H	1988 L	2008 I
1929 B	1949 F	1969 C	1989 G	2009 D
1930 C	1950 G	1970 D	1990 A	2010 E
1931 D	1951 A	1971 E	1991 B	2011 F
1932 L	1952 I	1972 M	1992 J	2012 N
1933 G	1953 D	1973 A	1993 E	2013 B
1934 A	1954 E	1974 B	1994 F	2014 C
1935 B	1955 F	1975 C	1995 G	2015 D
1936 J	1956 N	1976 K	1996 H	2016 L
1937 E	1957 B	1977 F	1997 C	2017 G
1938 F	1958 C	1978 G	1998 D	2018 A
1939 G	1959 D	1979 A	1999 E	2019 B

MONTHS

	J	F	M	A	M	J	J	A	S	O	N	D
A	1	4	4	7	2	5	7	3	6	1	4	6
B	2	5	5	1	3	6	1	4	7	2	5	7
C	3	6	6	2	4	7	2	5	1	3	6	1
D	4	7	7	3	5	1	3	6	2	4	7	2
E	5	1	1	4	6	2	4	7	3	5	1	3
F	6	2	2	5	7	3	5	1	4	6	2	4
G	7	3	3	6	1	4	6	2	5	7	3	5
H	1	4	5	1	3	6	1	4	7	2	5	7
I	2	5	6	2	4	7	2	5	1	3	6	1
J	3	6	7	3	5	1	3	6	2	4	7	2
K	4	7	1	4	6	2	4	7	3	5	1	3
L	5	1	2	5	7	3	5	1	4	6	2	4
M	6	2	3	6	1	4	6	2	5	7	3	5
N	7	3	4	7	2	5	7	3	6	1	4	6

DAYS

	1	2	3	4	5	6	7
Monday	1						
Tuesday	2	1					
Wednesday	3	2	1				
Thursday	4	3	2	1			
Friday	5	4	3	2	1		
Saturday	6	5	4	3	2	1	
Sunday	7	6	5	4	3	2	1
Monday	8	7	6	5	4	3	2
Tuesday	9	8	7	6	5	4	3
Wednesday	10	9	8	7	6	5	4
Thursday	11	10	9	8	7	6	5
Friday	12	11	10	9	8	7	6
Saturday	13	12	11	10	9	8	7
Sunday	14	13	12	11	10	9	8
Monday	15	14	13	12	11	10	9
Tuesday	16	15	14	13	12	11	10
Wednesday	17	16	15	14	13	12	11
Thursday	18	17	16	15	14	13	12
Friday	19	18	17	16	15	14	13
Saturday	20	19	18	17	16	15	14
Sunday	21	20	19	18	17	16	15
Monday	22	21	20	19	18	17	16
Tuesday	23	22	21	20	19	18	17
Wednesday	24	23	22	21	20	19	18
Thursday	25	24	23	22	21	20	19
Friday	26	25	24	23	22	21	20
Saturday	27	26	25	24	23	22	21
Sunday	28	27	26	25	24	23	22
Monday	29	28	27	26	25	24	23
Tuesday	30	29	28	27	26	25	24
Wednesday	31	30	29	28	27	26	25
Thursday		31	30	29	28	27	26
Friday			31	30	29	28	27
Saturday				31	30	29	28
Sunday					31	30	29
Monday						31	30
Tuesday							31

THE WOBBLY WEEK

The week has not always consisted of seven days except among the Jews. The Greeks had three ten-day weeks in a month; the Romans had an eight-day week. After the French Revolution, the French tried a ten-day week. That experiment lasted ten years, until 1806. In 1929 the Soviet Union tested a shifting four-day work week with the fifth day a day of rest, but it too was abandoned after only two years.

Sunday is named for the Sun and Monday for the Moon. The other days of the week are named for various ancient gods: Four days of the week are named for Norse gods and one for a Roman god:

Tuesday for Tiv (the ancient German name for Mars)
Wednesday for Woden (Mercury)
Thursday for Thor (Jupiter)
Friday for Frigga (Venus)
Saturday for the Roman god Saturn, father of Jupiter

3. TELLING TIME BY THE SUN

Our ancestors were mostly concerned with sunrise, noon and sunset. For those, they watched the Sun—or the shadow cast by trees or rocks or the distant hills.

For at least ten and perhaps as much as twenty centuries, measuring the shadow cast by the Sun was an important method of telling time. The sundial is mentioned in the Bible in an incident scholars say took place in 741 BC.

In Chaucer's *Canterbury Tales,* written about 1400, the Parson estimates the time on the basis of his height and the length of his shadow. And characters in several of Shakespeare's plays use sundials.

SUNDIAL TIMELINE

1500 BC	Fragment of earliest known sundial (now in a Berlin museum)
900s BC	Egyptians make T-shaped shadow timetellers with hours marked along their length
600s BC	Greek philosopher and astronomer Anaximander of Miletus introduces sundial into Greece
600–300 BC	An instrument is devised that doesn't have to be turned in the afternoon
200s BC	Chaldean astronomer Berossus describes the first hemispheric sundial
200 BC	Sundial commonplace in Rome
100	Sundial with gnomon (the arm on a sundial) tilted at an angle according to latitude
1528	Portable sundial with 10 faces, each at a different latitude

Where Does My Shadow Go?

Our ancestors told the time by the shadows made by the Sun. But why do we sometimes see a shadow and at other times "there's none of him at all?"

You need:

flashlight or a lamp   darkened room

What to do:

In a darkened room, place the lighted lamp or flashlight about five feet (1½m) from the wall You can hang up a sheet if the wall is a dark color. Stand behind the lamp. Do you cast a shadow? Now stand between the lamp and the wall. Then move closer to the wall.

What happens:

You don't cast a shadow when you stand behind the light. You cast a big shadow when you are near the light and far from the wall. As you move farther from the light, the shadow becomes smaller.

Why:

You cast a shadow by blocking the rays of light. As you move away from the source of light, your shadow becomes smaller because you cut off fewer rays of light. Any object that won't permit light to shine through creates a shadow, an area of lessened light.

Why Am I Sometimes Very Tall?

This simple experiment shows *how* the length of a shadow changes when the source of light changes position.

You need:

2 pencils   spool of thread
sheet of paper   flashlight

What to do:
Stand one of the pencils in the center of the spool over the sheet of paper. Darken the room and hold the flashlight at different angles above the pencil. Record the length of each shadow.

What happens:
When the flashlight is high and right above the pencil, the shadow is short. When the light is low and at a slant, the shadow is long.

Why:
When the light is low and at a slant, the shadow is long because few rays of light pass through. This shows us why the shadows at the North Pole are longer than those at the equator. The Sun hits Earth directly at the equator and indirectly at the Poles.

Shadow Watch

At what time of day is the shadow the shortest? You can find out by watching the shadow cast by the Sun—in the same way our distant ancestors did!

You need:
tree or lamppost
chalk or stones
pencil and paper
clock
tape measure

What to do:
Identify a nearby tree or a lamppost that is in sunlight much of the day.

Using either small stones or chalk, mark off the shadow it casts right after you get up in the morning. Measure the shadow's length. Then do the same thing at noon or, if your area is on Daylight Savings Time (Summer Time), an hour later. Finally, mark the shadow cast late in the afternoon toward sunset and measure it.

What happens:
The shadow is shortest at noon. The shadows cast in the early morning and late afternoon are both much longer.

Why:
The Sun is highest in the sky at noon and therefore casts the shortest shadow. However, your clock and the Sun may have a difference of opinion about when it is noon. (See 34 to find out why.)

Shadow Timepiece

The earliest timetelling device, a crude forerunner of the more accurate sundial, was the Egyptian shadow clock. It dates from between the 10th and 8th centuries BC and was made of stone. You can make your own from materials you have around the house.

You need:

2 empty milk cartons   index card
glue or tape   marker or crayon
scissors

What to do:

Place one of the milk cartons on its side. Glue or tape an index card or a piece of cardboard one inch (2½cm) from the top of the short flat end of the carton. Hold the second carton perpendicular to the first and attach it to the free end of the index card, as in the illustration. In the morning, go outdoors and place the shadow clock level with the upper carton pointing east. In the afternoon, turn the timeteller around so that it points west. Check with

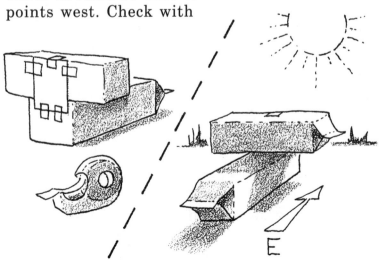

your clock every hour and mark where the shadow falls.

What happens:

The shadow shortens as it gets to be lunch time and lengthens again toward dinner time. And the distances from one hour to the next differ! The shadows are farther apart from one another early and late in the day and closer during the middle of the day.

Why:

Only at the equator will the spaces allotted to hours be exactly equal because the sunlight hits Earth directly. Unlike the day and the year, which are dictated by the revolution of Earth on its axis and around the Sun, the hour is a division devised by people. The day runs from midnight to midnight but it could be divided—and has been—into 20 parts or six parts or three parts instead of 24 hours. Early Egyptians didn't talk about two or three o'clock. They agreed to meet when the shadow was, for instance, four steps long.

What's the Angle?

In about the first century, it was discovered that a slanting object cast a shadow that kept more accurate time than an object that stood straight up. This was especially true if the object, known as the *gnomon,* slanted at the same angle as the latitude of the place where it was being used. In that case, its direction was the same at any hour of the day, regardless of the season of the year.

The term *gnomon* comes from the Greek word which means "know," so named because it "knew" the time.

You need:

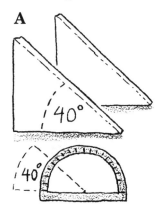

2 pieces of heavy cardboard approx. 6" × 8" (15 × 20cm)

4" (10cm) stick or pencil

protractor

atlas

scissors

paste

watch

marker or pencil

What to do:

In an atlas, look up the latitude of your town—that's its distance north or south of the equator. Subtract it from 90° (for example, 90° − 50° = 40°). From one of the pieces of cardboard, cut two wedge shapes with that angle; see illustration A.

A

On a second cardboard, **B** draw a line parallel to and 1" (2.5cm) away from the long edge, as in illustration B.

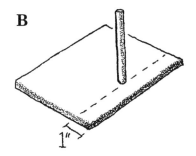

Paste the 4" (10cm) stick at right angles to the cardboard through the center of the line. With the protractor, divide the space above the line into 12 angles of 15° each. Label the middle line 12 and the bottom lines 6. Then fill in the other numbes, as in illustration C.

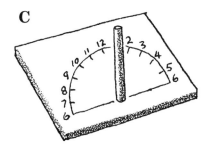

Paste the cardboards to the wedges so that the boards touch at one edge and the hour lines of the upper board point away from the free edge. See illustration D.

Set the sundial level. Place the edge where the two boards meet so that they run east and west. A simple way of orienting the sundial is to set it up at noon and indicate where the shadow falls. Check the sundial each hour, marking the spot where the shadow falls with a marker or pencil.

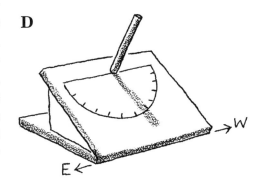

What happens:
The shadow of the stick will point to the time.

Why:
You have set up the sundial so that the gnomon is in the same direction as Earth's axis and the upper board is parallel to the ground at the North Pole.

But it will not always agree with your clock.

WHY THE DIFFERENCE?

L.A.T., local apparent time, is time measured by the actual movement of Earth and the Sun. It differs from season to season and from place to place. It is the time measured by the sundial.

L.M.T., local mean time, measures the average speed at which the Sun rotates and Earth spins in its orbit. Our clocks and watches show local mean time.

Hand Dial

A sixteenth century German woodcut shows a unique portable dial that requires no special equipment. If you know the latitude of your area (see p. 28), you can tell the time without a watch or sundial. Actually, you can be a human timepiece.

You need:
small stick or pencil
your two hands
sunny day

What to do:
Look up the latitude of your area in an atlas or on a globe. Using your left hand in the morning and your right hand in the afternoon, hold the stick with your thumb. Tilt the stick at an angle approximately equal to the angle of latitude of your area, as in the illustration below. Hold your left hand straight up toward the west. Hold your right hand straight up toward the east.

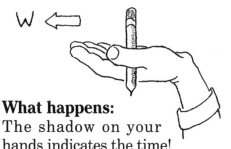

What happens:
The shadow on your hands indicates the time!

Why:
You have made the pencil into a gnomon and angled it parallel to Earth's axis, as in the last experiment. But remember, your hand sundial may not agree with your clock. See pages 30 and 34.

Noon Marks

Instead of noting time by the position of a shadow, you can note it from the position of a small beam of light. It is easy but it takes patience—and two seasons.

You need:
a window that faces south
piece of black paper
punch or nail
masking tape
pencil

What to do:
Punch a hole about ¼" (½cm) in diameter in a piece of black contact paper or a piece of cardboard. Fit the paper over a window that faces south. With a dot of masking tape, mark the spot on the floor where a sunbeam hits at noon on a winter's day. Then mark it again at noon on a summer's day. Connect the two spots on the floor.

What happens:

Whenever the sunbeam crosses the line, it will be the local apparent noon, the time the Sun (not your watch) says it is noon. Sun time and your watch will only agree on April 16, June 14, September 2 and December 25.

Why:

Days measured by the Sun differ in length. There are two reasons: (1) Earth moves faster when closer to the Sun and (2) the Earth's path around the Sun is an ellipse rather than a circle.

NOON HOLES

Noon marks can still be seen in Europe's ancient cathedrals. In the Duomo in Milan, a church dating back to 1380, there is a Sun hole on one wall near the ceiling and signs of the Zodiac indicating the months on its marble floor. Posted on a bulletin board is a daily schedule of times the Sun will shine on each month's symbol.

Time Zones

The difference between Sun time and clock time depends on where in a time zone you are located. You can see this for yourself with the shadow time-piece. See page 70 for an explanation of time zones.

You need:
stick (or long string with a rock tied to one end)

What to do:
Place a stick straight up in the ground. When its shadow is shortest, check your watch.

What happens:
If you live in the eastern edge of your time zone, the Sun at noon is earlier than the clock reading. If you live in the western edge of your time zone, the Sun at noon is later than the clock reading. If you are on Daylight Saving Time (Summer Time; see page 75), you need to take that into account—your clock will read before or after 1 o'clock.

Why:
The geographical region in which the same time is used is large. It is only in the middle of the region that the Sun will be highest in the sky at noon on our clocks.

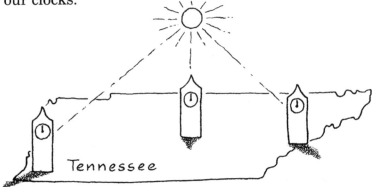

Tennessee

THE FICKLE HOUR

We now divide the day into 24 equal parts throughout the year, but it was not always like that. The Egyptians divided daylight into 12 parts and the darkness into 12 parts, but during the summer when days were longer, they lengthened the daylight divisions.

The Babylonians did the same thing, but they divided the day into 12 hours instead of 24. They had two systems. One of them began at midnight and divided the day into six parts, each with 60 subdivisions. The other measured the start of day from sunset and split it into 12 divisions with 30 subdivisions.

Early Hebrews divided the day into six parts, three light and three dark. While the Chinese adopted an equal hour system by the 4th century BC, Europeans changed the length of hours according to the seasons until the 14th century. The Japanese continued to have variable hours until 1868.

4. CLOUDY DAY AND NIGHT TIMETELLERS

Sundials, of course, were of no use on cloudy days and at night. People used many kinds of household materials to measure time on those days and at night. They tied knots in ropes to mark the hours, and burned measured quantities of oil, incense, and specially prepared candles.

CLOUDY DAY TIMELINE

1400 BC	Egyptians and Mesopotamians produce glass
1450 BC	Egyptians devise water clock
700 BC	Assyrians acquire water clock
38 BC	Plato adds alarm to water clock
200s BC	Hourglass invented in Alexandria
250 BC	Alexandrian engineer Ctesibius adds gears connected to a pointer on a drum indicating time
150 BC	Pliny writes that the water clock replaced the sundial as official timepiece
50	Athens acquires water solar clock
725	Buddhist monk T-Xing and Chinese engineer Liang-Zen build a water clock with an escapement used to power various astronomical devices
875	Calibrated candles mark the passage of time

Candle Timekeeper

Religious candles are reminders of the candle timekeepers of old, which date back to the 9th century.

You need:

2 white candles (not the tapered kind)

4 or 5 2-inch (5cm) lengths of heavy thread

2 candle holders

2 plates

4 or 5 bolts or paper clips

ruler

clock

What to do:

Attach a bolt or clip to one end of each 2-inch length of heavy thread.

Even out the candles by cutting or burning off the tips. Measure the candles. Jot down the results. Then insert one of the candles in a holder and place it on a plate. (Work near a sink—with adult supervision if that is the rule in your house.) Light the candle in the holder and let it burn for ten minutes. Then blow out the flame. Measure the candle again and figure out how much of the candle burned in 10 minutes. Loop one of the lengths of string around the second candle at the 10-minute mark and secure it with a knot. Mark off the rest of the first candle in 10-minute segments. Measure it each time and wrap a length of string, with a bolt or clip attached, at the proper spot on the second candle.

Depending on the size of your candle, you may be able to use more or less than four lengths of string. Insert the second candle in a candle holder, place it on a plate, and light the wick. Check your watch every time you hear the clang of the bolt or clip.

What happens:

Every ten minutes, you will be alerted by an "alarm" as the thread burns off and the clip or bolt hits the plate.

Water Clock

One of the most ingenious of cloudy day timekeepers was the water clock, the *clepsydra*. It originated in Egypt and Babylon and came into use about a thousand years after the sundial.

The Egyptians poked a small hole in a large clay bowl—wide at the top and narrow at the bottom—that was marked with horizontal lines on the inside, one for each hour. As water leaked out, they could tell how much time had passed by looking at the lines and the water left in the pot.

You can make your own clepsydra with a plastic container.

You need:

plastic container or cup
small piece of tape (optional)
large pot (or use of the sink)
color marker
punch or nail
pitcher of water
clock or timer
paper and pencil

What to do:

(1) Use your marker to make 3 or 4 lines equally distant from one another around the inside of the container. Then punch a small hole in the bottom of the container. Cover the hole with a piece of tape or hold your finger over it. Fill the carton with water. Place the carton over a large pot (or the sink), uncover the hole and see how long it takes the carton to empty. Jot down your findings.

(2) Fill the container again. This time note how long it takes to get to each of the lines you've drawn, as well as how long it takes for the container to empty.

What happens:
It takes the same amount of time to empty during the two trials, but the time to move from one line to the next differs.

Why:
The water pressure lessens as the water escapes, and so the water runs out more slowly than when the container is full.

You may want to experiment with cartons of different sizes and shapes. See if it makes a difference using hot water or ice-cold water from the refrig-erator.

NOT QUITE PERFECT

Unlike the candle or rope clocks, the water clock could be used over and over. But there were problems. Although it didn't need the Sun to show how much time had passed, it was not really an all-weather timepiece. When it was very cold, the water would freeze; when it was very hot the water would evaporate too quickly. And when it was dirty, whether from human or natural causes, it slowed down.

Having It Both Ways

A more accurate water clock has water flowing in and out of containers at the same time.

You need:

yardstick   glass bowl or a
masking tape   pot
2 heavy paper cups
punch or nail
water source
marker
watch

What to do:
Punch a small
hole in the bottom of
the paper cups. Hold the yardstick up and
tape the cups to it, as in the illustration. Tape
the yardstick to the side of a large pot or bowl with
the cups facing inward so that they are over the pot.

Cover the hole in the top cup with a piece of tape.
Fill the cup with water. Then place it under a slow-
running faucet as you uncover the hole.

Every five minutes, use tape or a marker to indicate the water line in the bottom cup and the one in
the bowl or pot.

What happens:
The water flows out at a regular rate and the marks
are equally distant from one another.

Why:
Because the amount of water that flows in comes
from a cup that is always kept full, the water pressure remains the same and therefore the water
flows out at the same rate.

Hourglass Timekeepers

Hourglass timers were once engaged in serious jobs. They timed sermons, speeches, court presentations. Four-hour models were used aboard ship to measure watches right up to the late 18th century, when accurate ship chronometers were invented. Now, the most common task of the hourglass is to time boiled eggs.

You need:

2 small clear jars (babyfood or jelly size)
heavy paper or cardboard
masking tape
salt or sand
nail or punch
scissors
clock or watch

What to do:

Cut a circle out of a piece of heavy paper or cardboard to fit the mouth of the jars. Punch a small hole in the center of the circle with a nail or a paper punch. Place a few ounces of sand or salt in one of the jars and cover it with the disk. Tape the second jar to the first, mouth to mouth. Make sure they are taped securely. Then turn the jars upside down. and time how long it takes for the top jar to empty.

Now make the hole larger and change the amount of sand. Time these.

What happens:
By making the hole larger or smaller—or changing the amount of sand or salt—you can change the time it takes to empty the top jar.

Why:
Gravity is what forces the sand to drop at a steady rate. The advantages of the hourglass over the water clock? It is portable—no sloshing water—and weather does not affect it. You can use it over and over and time longer periods—if you just keep track of how many times you turn it over. This "minute glass" should be fun and you may even find it useful.

A KNOTTY PROBLEM

For many years, it was the practice at sea to throw overboard a thin rope weighted at one end with a piece of wood and knotted at regular intervals. A seaman would hold the rope as it was dragged through the water and feel how many knots passed through his hands during the time it took for a timed sandglass to empty. In this way, he estimated the speed or "knots" at which the ship was moving. Nautical speed is still measured in knots.

Invent Your Own Clock

Timetellers have ranged from natural phenomena to manmade devices, from primitive to sophisticated, from simple to complex. The writer Albert Camus tells of an old man who thought a watch a silly gadget and an unnecessary expense. He devised his own "clock" designed to indicate the only times he was interested in. He worked out the times for meals with two saucepans, one of which was always filled with peas when he woke in the morning. He filled the other, pea by pea, at a constant, carefully regulated speed. Every 15 pots of peas it was feeding time!

Fifth graders from the Fieldston School in Riverdale, New York, invented their own timers—one made a fizzy alarm clock using vinegar dripping into baking soda, another timed how long it took heat to blow up a balloon.

Can you devise a "clock" from items around the house or activities you do often?

5. TELLING TIME BY THE STARS

While the ancient Egyptians built sundials to keep track of daylight hours, during the night they measured the movement of the stars across certain portions of the sky.

They associated their goddess Isis, "the lady of all the elements, the beginning of all time" with the brightest star in the night sky, Sirius. They built temples facing the point on the eastern horizon where Sirius first appeared before sunrise. Ancient Egyptian astronomers, tracking Sirius for their calendar, started a new year at the first new moon following this appearance of Sirius—and all awaited the annual floods that irrigated the land.

In the Northern Hemisphere, a February evening is a good time to look for Sirius to the side and a little below the group of stars known as Orion the Hunter. Face south at about 9 PM. Orion is high in the winter sky but not visible in northern skies during the summer.

Using the line of Orion's belt as a guide, look southeast for the Dog Star.

STAR TIMELINE

3000 BC — Earliest Babylonian astronomical records

300 BC — Chinese astronomers chart position of stars

280 BC — Aristarchus suggests Earth orbits the Sun

140 — Ptolemy contends that planets orbit Earth, a theory accepted for 1500 years

500 — Astrolabe, developed in ancient Greece, is used for reckoning time and measuring the position of heavenly bodies. Later, mariners use it in navigation

1543 — Nicholas Copernicus, a Polish priest, publishes theory that the Sun is the center of the universe. Idea banned as challenging the Bible

1608 — Hans Lippershey of the Netherlands invents first telescope

1609 — Galileo Galilei confirms Copernicus' theory but is eventually forced to recant

1620s — German mathematician Johannes Kepler proves planets move around the Sun

1668 — Isaac Newton invents a reflector telescope with a curved mirror replacing one lens

1739 — Sextant is invented by Thomas Godfrey and John Hadley.

Cereal Box Planetarium

You can make your own "planetarium" by creating a model of a cluster of stars you will see in the sky.

You need:
round box (the type that oatmeal or raisins are packaged in)
piece of tracing paper
pencil or pen
flashlight
small nail or nail file

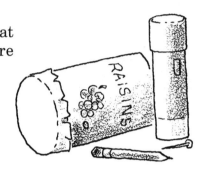

What to do:
Make a circle of tracing paper or other transparent paper to fit the bottom of the box. Then copy the illustration of the Big Dipper, the Pole Star, and Cassiopeia shown below onto the thin piece of paper. Next paste the sheet to the bottom of the box. The stars will show through the thin paper. With the nail or other sharp point, punch holes through the box at each star.

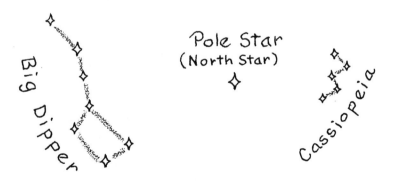

Take the planetarium to a dark room and stand facing one of the room's walls. At the open end of the

box tilt a flashlight so that it shines against the side.
Turn the box slowly.

What happens:

You will get an enlarged image on the wall. When you turn the box, you will see the various positions of the stars as they seem to revolve.

Why:

Earth rotates on its axis, so the constellations appear to circle around the Pole Star, which remains at the same place in the sky. Therefore, you see these constellations in all positions—on their sides or even upside down. The "W" shape of Cassiopeia becomes an "M" depending on when it appears above the Pole Star.

THE SKY AS COMPASS

If you are ever lost in a forest at night, you can use the sky to find your way. Face the Pole Star, which is the brightest star in the northern sky, and you are facing north. Look 180° across the sky to the horizon is south. East is 90° to the right and west 90° to the left.

Star Map

Draw a star map of the constellations that circle around the Pole Star and use it to note the changes in the sky from hour to hour.

You need:
circle of cardboard or plastic
flashlight
red cellophane and tape (optional)

What to do:
Copy this illustration onto your circle of cardboard or plastic.

Tape the cellophane over your flashlight.

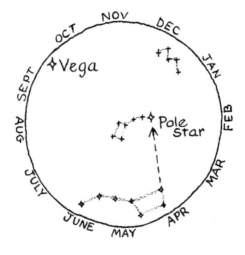

(1) At 9 o'clock on a dry moonless night, take your star map and the flash outdoors. (The red covering will prevent it from being too bright for you to see the stars.) Rotate the chart so that the month in which you are observing is on the top. Hold the chart above your head and look for the same pattern in the sky.

(2) On another night, go out at 7 o'clock or at 10 o'clock and match the star map with the sky.

What happens:

At 7 o'clock you have to turn the chart one month clockwise to match the sky. At 10 o'clock you have to turn it a half-month counterclockwise.

Why:

The Pole Star remains at approximately the same place in the sky—far, far away but directly above Earth's North Pole. This is because Earth's axis points to it throughout the year.

But all the other stars and constellations seem to wander around the Pole Star once a day, *moving counterclockwise*. As Earth rotates, it looks as if the entire sky is rotating, though the stars do not change position relative to each other. Since one turn of Earth takes only 23 hours and 56 minutes, a star seems to rise and set about four minutes earlier than the day before. This add ups to 2 hours (30 × 4 = 120 minutes) in a month and, of course, one hour in half a month.

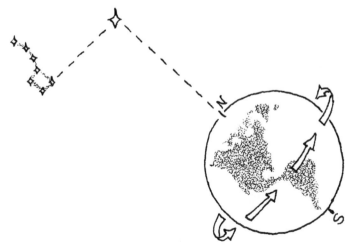

SOME TIME-TELLING STARS

Orion is one of 88 constellations—groups of stars that long ago people named for heroes and gods and animals that they thought the patterns looked like. We still use many of these names both in Latin and the English translation. And we still use the stars as a calendar and a direction finder.

The only place we can see all 88 constellations during the course of a year is the equator. In other latitudes, you can see perhaps 60 at different times, and about 24 at any one time.

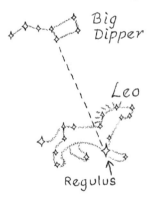

In the United States, Canada, the U.K. and Europe, you can see the constellation of Leo, the Lion, with the bright star Regulus high up in the sky at about 9 PM in the middle of April.

In August, as it gets dark, high in the southeast section of the sky you will see three bright stars—the Summer Triangle. Directly overhead are Vega, in the constellation Lyra, the Harp; Deneb of the constellation Cygnus, the Swan; and Altair of the constellation Aquila, the Eagle.

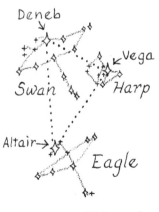

Summer Triangle

Cassiopeia

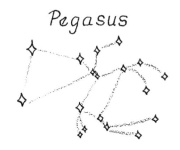

Pegasus

In the evening skies of October, just below the W-shaped constellation Cassiopeia, you will find four bright stars arranged in a square making up the body of an upside-down horse with wings, the constellation Pegasus, the flying horse.

In the Southern Hemisphere, the Southern Cross (the Crux) is the easiest constellation to recognize. You can see it in the evening skies of Miami and the Florida Keys in May and June, but its four stars are always visible below the equator. Looking south, observers in Australia, southern Africa and South America can see the Crux just below the

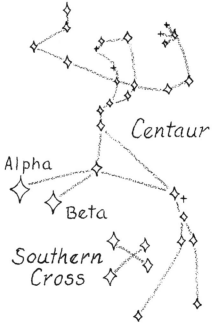

Centaur

Alpha

Beta

Southern Cross

two bright stars Alpha and Beta Centauri. Some think it looks more like a kite than a cross.

Star Time

Stars tell us the time and direction on land, on sea, and in the air. You can have fun estimating the time by observing certain stars.

You need:

3 pieces of cardboard   punch or nail
marker   fastener
compass (optional)   flashlight
ruler   sheet of paper
scissors   paste or glue
tape

What to do:

Mark out circles on two of the pieces of cardboard. Make one circle about 8" (20cm) in diameter. Make the other 1" (2.5cm) smaller with four 3" (7.5cm) triangles sticking out as in C. Cut out the two disks.

On the larger cardboard disk draw two ¼" circles around the outer rim. Mark the outer circle with the months of the year. Mark the inner circle with the days of the month.

A

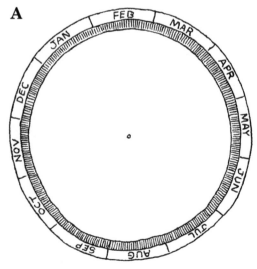

From the sheet of paper, cut out an oval 3¾" (9.5cm) deep and 4" (10cm) wide. Copy the sky map in illustration B.

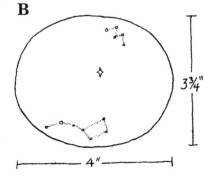

B

3¾"

4"

Hold the larger disk so that September is on top. Paste the sky map to the inner circle above the days of March.

On the smaller disk, 1" from the bottom, mark out an oval, also 3¾" deep and 4" wide. Cut the oval section out.

Around the edge of the smaller disk draw a clock face like the one in illustration C. Notice that the numbers, like the stars, go in the opposite direction from an ordinary clock and cover 24 hours instead of 12.

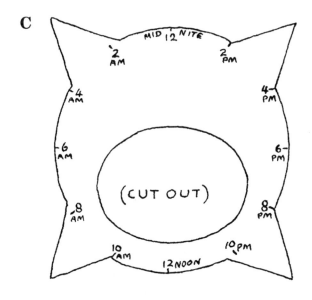

C

MID 12 NITE

2 AM   2 PM

4 AM   4 PM

6 AM   6 PM

(CUT OUT)

8 AM   8 PM

10 AM   10 PM

12 NOON

Place the smaller disk on top of the larger disk so that you can see the map through the "window" of the smaller disk.

Tape the tips of the triangles of the smaller disk to the corners of the third cardboard. Punch a hole through the center of all three cardboards. Fit the fastener through the three center holes.

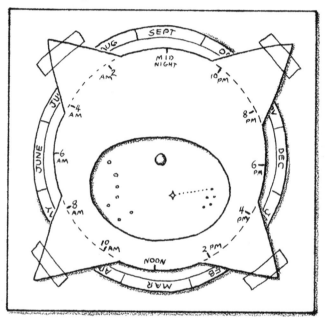

On a clear, preferably moonless, night, pick a spot where street lights, houses and trees don't obstruct your view.

Face north and look for the Big Dipper and Cassiopeia. Two pointer stars of the Big Dipper point to a fairly bright star, the Pole Star (Polaris)—also known as the North Star—which is halfway between the Big Dipper and Cassiopeia. At a latitude of 40° (New York, Denver, Salt Lake City), it is almost halfway up in the sky. The farther north

(London's latitude is 50°) you are, the higher up the Pole Star will be; the farther south (New Orleans is 30°), the lower it will be.

Rotate your Star Timeteller until it looks like the sky.

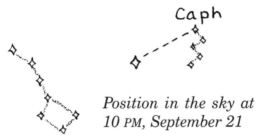

Caph

Position in the sky at 10 PM, September 21

Draw an imaginary line from Polaris to Caph, one of the bright stars of Cassiopeia.

For each week after September 21 subtract ½ hour; for each week earlier add ½ hour. If you are on Daylight Savings Time, add an hour.

What happens:
The imaginary line acts as the star clock's hour hand. With a little simple arithmetic, you can find the approximate time.

Why:
You add and subtract depending on when you observe the stars because the solar day is longer than the star day. The star clock runs too fast. As we have seen. it gains four minutes every day. In a week it gains about a half hour (7 × 4 = 28 minutes); in a month it gains about 2 hours (30 × 4 = 120 minutes). Since Earth is rotating counterclockwise, it will be earlier when you observe *after* September 21, so you subtract. And it will be later *before* September 21, so you add.

6. MECHANICAL CLOCKS

A kind of mechanical timeteller existed in the late 13th or early 14th century. Housed on a high bell tower, it used a heavy falling weight tied to a rope that was wound around a huge revolving drum. It had no dials and, at first, no means of striking, but it could indicate important times by means of a moving figure called a jack. It alerted the keeper of the clock, usually a monk, to sound a bell. The word *clock* comes from the Latin word *clocca*, which means bell. Up until this time, any instrument that measured time was known as an *horologium* (hour teller).

Huge public clocks, which struck the hours but did not have a face with hands, appeared in Italian towns starting in the 14th century. Many of these—and some still exist—used a variety of jacks for entertainment.

Clocks made for royalty were even more elaborate. France's Louis XIV had a clock with models of several kings of Europe, who bowed to him before striking the hour with canes.

The cuckoo clock, with its carved wooden bird that pops out to "sing" the time, first appeared in Germany in 1730.

MECHANICAL TIMELINE

1320 — weight-driven mechanical clocks used
1350 — public clocks in European towns
1510 — portable spring-driven clocks invented
1583 — Galileo Galilei of Rome shows that a pendulum swings at a constant rate
1656 — Christian Huygens designs a pendulum clock
1660 — Huygens and Robert Hooke invent the spiral hairspring
1668 — Boston has the first town clock in Colonial America
1675 — grandfather clocks available
1676 — minute hands and crystal covers added to watches
1725 — Nicholas Faceis of Basel adds jeweled bearings to reduce friction
1730 — cuckoo clocks made in the Black Forest
1773 — Englishman John Harrison invents a seagoing chronometer
1803 — Eli Terry of Connecticut begins clock mass production
1824 — "time ball" standardizes timekeeping in some towns
1875 — stem-wound watches replace watches with keys
1884 — standardized time zones established

Yo-Yo Clock

If you think about how a yo-yo spins when you unwind its cord, you'll have an idea of how the earliest mechanical clocks worked. The energy of falling weights suspended from a drum were its source of its power.

You need:
length of heavy thread or cord
empty thread spool
heavy button or a washer

What to do:
Tie one end of the cord to a washer or heavy button. Tie the other end around the spool and wind it up. (1) Turn the spool so that the weight hangs down, as in the illustration. (2) Rewind the spool. Again turn the spool so that the weight hangs down, but this time keep tapping the edge of the spool quickly with your finger.

What happens:

When the weight falls, the cord unwinds and the spool turns quickly. But when you tap the spool, your finger acts as a brake. The taps stop the spool and the weight falls in small jerks with a slow and steady regular rhythm.

Why:

The falling weight supplied the energy to turn the spool while the tapping finger regulated it. Clocks worked in the same way by means of a device called an *escapement*. The escapement made sure the weight fell slowly and steadily and prevented the drum from rotating too fast and using up all the energy of the weight too quickly.

These early clocks, installed in bell towers, weighed hundreds of pounds and fell distances of more than 30 feet (9m) but were highly inaccurate.

SUNDIALS VS. MECHANICAL CLOCKS

Early mechanical clocks were inaccurate and therefore sundials were used to regulate them until the advent of electrical clocks in the late 19th century!

ABOUT GEARS

GET ADULT HELP

Gears are wheels with notches or teeth. Small gears are called pinions. Wheels with 20 or more teeth are called gears. Large gears with an even greater number of teeth are called cogs.

The first clocks had a gear at each end of a spindle, the axle of the spool. The gear on the back of the spool axle meshed with a series of gears that regulated the unwinding of the cord. The other gear on the spool—the one on the front of the spool axis-controlled moving figures (called jacks), which beat on bells to sound the hours. Later this front gear turned a hand that showed the hour on a round dial.

You need:
3 bottle caps
block of wood
3 thin nails
hammer and nail
　or a punch

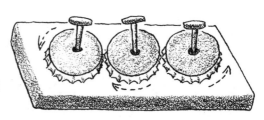

What to do:
Be sure the caps are not bent. Punch a hole through the center of each. Take care not to hurt your fingers—ask a parent for help if that is the rule in your house.

Place the caps on the block of wood close enough to one another so that they touch. Tack them down loosely with thin nails so that they turn easily.

Turn one of the caps with your finger and notice what happens to the others. Turn one of the caps in the opposite direction. Turn them slowly, then quickly.

What happens:
When you turn one cap, all three turn. But each gear turns in the opposite direction from the one next to it.

Why:
The ridges of each cap act like the teeth of a gear and interlock—mesh—with the ridges of the cap next to it. In addition to changing direction, gears change force or speed. Speed increases when a small gear is turned by a large one and force increases when a large gear is turned by a small one.

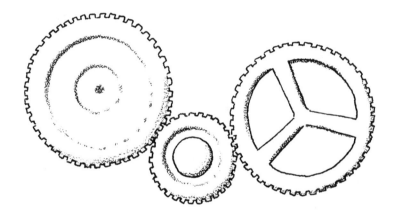

The set of gears of a clock changes slow turning into fast turning. It connects the axle to several wheels. As the axle turns, the wheels turn at different speeds. The regulator—the escapement—controls the turning of the fastest of the wheels. Two of the slower wheels turn the hands on the face of the clock.

Main features of all clocks are (1) a device that swings at a regular rate, (2) something that keeps the motion going by feeding energy to the swinging device, and (3) a means of counting and indicating the swings.

WHY CLOCKS COUNT TO 12

Do you know how hard it is to count the chimes when a clock strikes 12? Well, imagine what it would be like to have to count 24 chimes! That's what people had to do years ago when more and more clocks were striking the hour in village squares all over Europe. That's why, in the early 15th century, a double 12-hour system took the place of the 24-hour system in most countries.

This system of dividing the day into two set of twelve equal hours starting at midnight, scholars claim, originated in southern Germany, where the sale of locally made mechanical clocks was thriving.

Most military organizations and some parts of Europe, however, still use a 24-hour system starting at midnight. For instance, 12:59 AM is 0059; 1:00 AM is 0100; 12 noon is 1200; 12:59 PM is 1259; 1:00 PM is 1300; 10:59 PM is 2259. When you convert from a 12-hour clock to a 24-hour clock, the minutes are unchanged but you add 12 from 1:00 PM on. To convert from a 24-hour clock to a 12-hour system you just subtract 12 hours between 1300 and 2359 and add PM.

Military Time

Portable Timekeepers

In 1510, locksmith Peter Henlein of Nuremberg, substituting a small coiled spring for the huge weights, built the first table timekeepers that could be carried around. They were known as "Nuremberg Eggs" because of their oval shape. They were small enough to wear on a belt or on a chain around the neck, but they were not accurate enough to have a minute hand.

In 1660 Robert Hooke attached a small balance wheel to the mainspring, and a short, stiff hog's hair bristle to control the oscillations—the movements back and forth. Later, a fine steel wire was used instead of a bristle, but it continued to be known as the hairspring—and still is! All the mechanical watches to come were based on its design.

So, now the watch had (1) a mainspring, the source of energy; (2) an escapement and balance unit, which controlled the release of energy; and (3) two gear trains, one transmitting the energy and another controlling the movement of the hands. It also included a mechanism for winding the clock and a frame or case to protect it.

When you wind up a watch, you coil the spring tightly around the central shaft, which is held by a gear attached to a bar with projecting levers. As the housing turns around the shaft, the spring gradually unwinds. The gear attached to the housing drives other gears that move the hands of the watch.

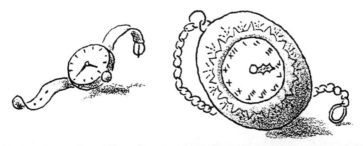

Jewels As Cushions

Sometime between the end of the 17th century and the beginning of the 18th century, Swiss watchmakers began to use chips of sapphires and rubies to ease the friction between various parts so they moved more smoothly and didn't wear out as fast. A 17-jeweled watch has 17 of these jeweled bearings, though now the "jewels" are probably synthetic. You can see the effect of the jeweled ball bearings by using a handful of marbles.

You need:

2 different-sized jar lids	tape
marbles	pencil
scissors	clay

What to do:

Turn both lids inside out. Tape the smaller lid to a table. Tape the pencil to the inside of the large jar lid. (1) Place the large lid on top of the small one and, using the pencil as lever, spin it. Note what happens. (2) Fill the small lid with marbles and then spin the large lid on it. Note what happens.

What happens:

(1) The top lid moves with difficulty. (2) The top lid spins easily.

Why:

When two things move in contact with one another, they resist moving. No two surfaces are completely smooth. The bumps of one surface catch on the bumps of the other. The resistance that results when the surfaces rub against each other is known as friction.

The amount of friction depends on the kinds of

surfaces as well as the force pressing them together. The rougher the surfaces, the greater the friction. Too much friction produces heat and wears away parts. The smooth, round marbles reduce the amount of friction. The contact between the moving parts and the marbles is very slight, and so the friction is very low. The tiny, hard gems in the watch reduce wear at the principal points of friction—the delicate axles around which the various wheels revolve. The more jeweled bearings in a watch, the longer it lasts.

ABOUT THE WORD "WATCH"

Where did the use of the word *watch* for a time-keeper come from? Some sources say it came from the Middle Ages, when the man who kept the night *watch* proclaimed "All's well!" and also announced the time. Others say it came about because people were at last able to *see* the time instead of merely hearing it announced by chimes or bells. Still others claim the word came from sailors who called their duty period—and still do—a *watch*.

Early watches were wound by a key inserted in a small hole under the back case. It wasn't until late in the 19th century that watches were wound by a stem. In self-winding watches the mainspring was tightened automatically by a weight on a rotor, a revolving part that responded to the slightest arm movements of the wearer.

Grandfather Clocks

In 1656 Christian Huygens van Zulicham, a Dutch scientist, invented the first pendulum clock. Based on the principle established by Galileo's experiments in 1583, the new clock was driven by a single weight—the bob—suspended on a long rope.

You need:
4 lengths of string or heavy thread:
   10" (25cm), 20" (50cm), 39" (97.5cm), 48" (120cm)
metal washers or coins or pebbles
clothes hanger or ceiling hook
watch with a second hand

What to do:
Tie a weight to the longest string and suspend it from a clothes hanger or a ceiling hook so that it hangs freely. Pull the string slightly to one side and let it swing. Count the number of swings it makes in 60 seconds. Then pull the string farther over to one side and let it swing again, counting the number of swings in 60 seconds. Add additional washers or coins or heavy pebbles and try swinging the string. Again count the number of swings made in 60 seconds. Jot down your results.

   Do the same thing with strings of different lengths— 10 inches, 20 inches, and finally 39 inches. In each case, note how many times the weight moves back and forth in 60 seconds and jot down the results.

What happens:
When the string is 39 inches long, the weight moves back and forth 60 times in one minute.

Why:
A pendulum takes the same length of time to make every swing no matter how far it travels or how heavy the weight at the end of it. But the longer the pendulum, the longer the time it takes to complete its swing; the shorter the pendulum the more quickly it travels back and forth. Since it takes one second for a length of string measuring 39 inches to swing back and forth, time can be measured with accuracy.

Because they were housed in tall wooden cases designed to hide the unattractive weights, pendulum clocks were known as *tall clocks*.

SECONDS

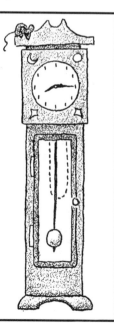

When pendulum clocks became more accurate, first minute hands and eventually second hands were added to clock faces. English physicist Robert Hooke was the first one to use the word *"second"* for one-sixtieth of a minute. Since there are 60 minutes in an hour, Hooke divided a minute into 60 parts, too. He called each part a *second* because he was dividing by 60 a *second* time.

Railroad Timetable

Barely more than 100 years ago every local community kept its own "official" time, calling it noon when the Sun was overhead. The time was announced to the people by a town clock, by a falling time ball in the center of town, or by a factory whistle. But when railroad travel became common, this was very confusing! The country needed a uniform schedule that everyone could follow. This brought about the uniform system of time zones that we have today. It met plenty of opposition, though, from many people who resented being "dictated to" by the railroads.

At a meeting on October 11, 1883, four time zones were established for the United States—Eastern, Central, Mountain, and Pacific—based on the 15° of longitude that the Sun travels in one hour.

The next year, by general international agreement, the entire world was divided into time zones—24 of them. Greenwich Mean Time, which had become the standard for all of the United Kingdom, was selected as the starting point from which international time zones and degrees of longitude were measured. Each zone was one hour earlier than the one immediately to the east.

The United States and its territories now have eight standard time zones including Atlantic Time for Puerto Rico and the Virgin Islands (one hour later than Eastern Standard), and Alaska, Hawaii—Aleutian, and Samoan Standard (one, two and three hours earlier respectively than Pacific Time). Canada's five time zones range from Atlantic time to Pacific–Yukon. Newfoundland is a half-hour later than Atlantic time.

Australia and other large land masses are also divided into time zones based primarily on longitude. Australia's three time zones range from Australian Western Standard Time in the city of Perth, to Australian Central Standard Time in the North Territory and North Australia, to Australian Eastern Standard Time in Queensland, Victoria and New South Wales, with Lord Howe Island a half-hour later. China has resisted zoning—all of that vast land uses Beijing Time, which coincides with that of Western Australia, 8 hours later than London. South Africa Standard Time is two hours later than London, and at noon in London it is midnight in New Zealand.

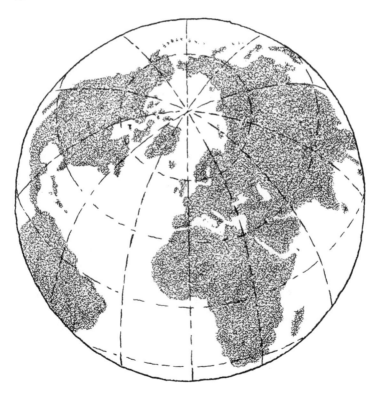

International Date Line

Do you know what the International Date Line is all about? Let's take a trip around the world and find out.

You need:

sheet of paper

pencil

tape

scissors

2 coins or pebbles

What to do:

Fold the paper in thirds lengthwise, as in A. Then fold in half three times, as in B (1, 2, 3).

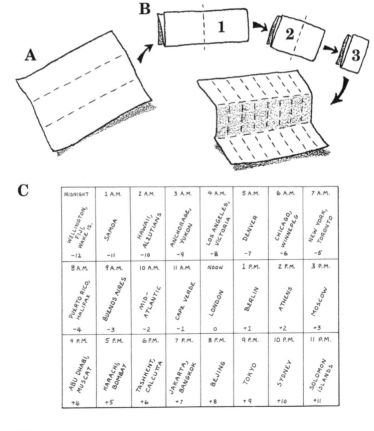

C	MIDNIGHT	1 A.M.	2 A.M.	3 A.M.	4 A.M.	5 A.M.	6 A.M.	7 A.M.
	WELLINGTON, FIJI, WAKE IS.	SAMOA	HAWAII, ALEUTIANS	ANCHORAGE, YUKON	LOS ANGELES, VICTORIA	DENVER	CHICAGO, WINNEPEG	NEW YORK, TORONTO
	-12	-11	-10	-9	-8	-7	-6	-5
	8 A.M.	9 A.M.	10 A.M.	11 A.M.	NOON	1 P.M.	2 P.M.	3 P.M.
	PUERTO RICO, HALIFAX	BUENOS AIRES	MID-ATLANTIC	CAPE VERDE	LONDON	BERLIN	ATHENS	MOSCOW
	-4	-3	-2	-1	0	+1	+2	+3
	4 P.M.	5 P.M.	6 P.M.	7 P.M.	8 P.M.	9 P.M.	10 P.M.	11 P.M.
	ABU DHABI, MUSCAT	KARACHI, BOMBAY	TASHKENT, CALCUTTA	JAKARTA, BANGKOK	BEIJING	TOKYO	SYDNEY	SOLOMON ISLANDS
	+4	+5	+6	+7	+8	+9	+10	+11

Number the strips and fill in the times and the names of the locales, as in illustration C.

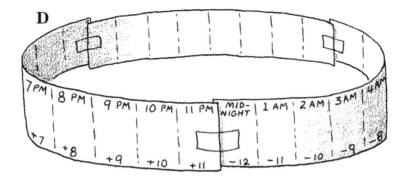

Then cut along the dotted lines. Tape the strips to one another, matching the numbers so that 5 follows 4 and – 5 follows – 4. Tape the ends (+ 12 and – 12) to one another. Each of the numbers represents a time zone one hour later or one hour earlier than Greenwich Mean Time in London.

Let us assume it is noon on Tuesday and our two coins are going on a trip around the globe. They both start in London, but one travels east to Berlin and one goes west towards New York. Their planes meet one another on a remote Pacific island, west of Eniwetok (a coral island in the Marshalls) and east of Fiji.

The one traveling eastward sets its clock ahead for each 15° of longitude to gain 12 hours. The one traveling westward sets its clock back one hour for each 15° so that it loses 12 hours.

What happens:

The two clocks differ by 24 hours in one calendar day.

The problem was solved by international agreement. At the International Date Line—at 180° of longitude, located in the Pacific Ocean—travelers are required to change the date. The one traveling east moves the calendar back a day; the one traveling west moves ahead a day.

The 180° meridian runs mostly through the open Pacific. But the date line zigzags to avoid a time change in populated areas—in the north to take the eastern tip of Siberia into the Siberian time system, to include a number of islands in the Hawaii—Aleutian time zone, and, farther south, to tie British-owned islands into the New Zealand time system.

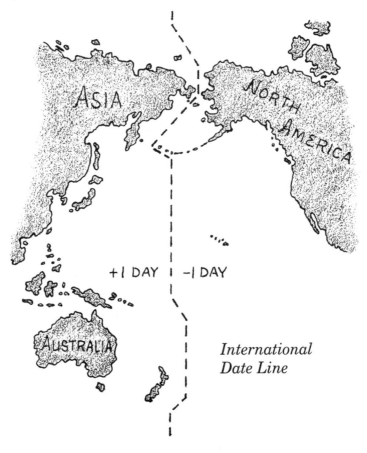

+1 DAY   −1 DAY

International Date Line

Daylight Savings Time

Daylight Savings Time, also known as Summer Time, is a system of putting clocks ahead an hour in the late spring and summer in order to extend daylight hours during the time people are awake. It was first suggested—perhaps as a joke—by Benjamin Franklin in 1784, but not until the 20th century was the idea put into effect. During World War I, Germany, the United States, Great Britain and Australia all adopted summer daylight savings time to conserve fuel by decreasing the use of artificial light. During World War II both the United States and Great Britain used it year-round—advancing clocks one hour during the winter and two during the summer.

Summer time observance was formally adopted as U.S. government policy in 1966, but even now it is not used in Indiana and Arizona. All of Canada observes Daylight Savings Time during the summer, but only some parts of Australia move clocks forward during their summer months starting the last Sunday in October.

AM and PM

Meridians are imaginary lines that run along Earth's surface from the North to the South Pole. When the Sun is over one of these meridians, for those on that meridian it is noon. East of that meridian it is post meridian, PM (after noon). West of that meridian it is ante meridian, AM (before noon).

7. SUPER CLOCKS

Though the mechanical clock and watch are still sold—and are sometimes even considered "status symbols"—more accurate and less expensive clocks and watches have been available for half a century. These are the electric and electronic timetellers. And, of course, for true accuracy, there is now the atomic clock, but this is neither inexpensive nor available for our night table or wrist—yet.

SUPER CLOCK TIMELINE

1800 — Alessandro Volta makes the first chemical battery
1821 — Michael Faraday uses a magnet to convert a wire carrying current to mechanical energy
1830 — Joseph Henry builds the first practical electric motor
1840 — Alexander Bain patents an electric clock
1881 — Pierre Curie discovers piezoelectric oscillation
1894 — Reliable master-clock system developed
1913 — Niels Bohr and Ernest T. Rutherford develop theory of structure of the atom
1918 — U.S. reliable AC current running at 60 cycles per second
1927 — U.K. reliable AC current running at 50 cycles per second
1929 — Warren Marrison invents quartz crystal clock
1949 — Harold Lyons of the U.S. National Bureau of Standards constructs first atomic clock using ammonia molecules
1955 — Dr. I. Essen and J. V. L. Parry in National Physical Lab in London develop atomic clock using cesium atom.
1957 — Electric wristwatches—battery replaces the spring
1958 — First integrated circuit (microchip)
1959 — Miniature tuning fork replaces the balance wheel
1965 — Transistorized battery clocks
1960s — LED (Light Emitting Diode)
1969 — First all-electronic watch with digital display
1967 — Frequency of vibrations of cesium atom is designated definition of a second
1970s — LCD (Liquid Crystal Display)

ELECTRIC CLOCKS

You don't have to wind an electric clock. The spring, the pendulum, and the escapement have been replaced by a motor, which is powered by the electricity from an electrical outlet or a battery.

The first patent for an electric clock was filed as early as 1840 by Alexander Bain, a Scotsman living in London. In 1894, Frank Hope-Jones and George Boswell built a reliable electric master-clock system that had a pendulum powered by an electric battery. The system was used to power networks of clocks in railway stations and factories.

But despite these inventions, you still couldn't plug a clock into an electrical outlet until 1918 in the United States and nine years later in Great Britain. Before that, and in some places for years afterward, homes and offices were wired only for direct current (DC), which has a steady flow in one direction. This couldn't be used for clocks because clocks needed current that flows in a circuit at regular intervals. That wasn't practical until a reliable alternating current (AC) was introduced. Then clockmakers were able to equip a clock with an electric motor with a rotor, a revolving part that spun at the same frequency as current from electricity-generating power stations (50 or 60 cycles a second).

Gears reduced the high speed to the slow turning needed by the hands of the clock.

An Electric Motor

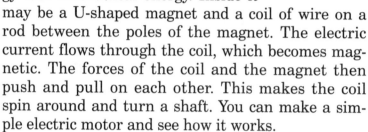

GET ADULT HELP

The electric motor in an electric clock or watch changes electric energy into mechanical energy. Inside it may be a U-shaped magnet and a coil of wire on a rod between the poles of the magnet. The electric current flows through the coil, which becomes magnetic. The forces of the coil and the magnet then push and pull on each other. This makes the coil spin around and turn a shaft. You can make a simple electric motor and see how it works.

You need:
piece of plywood approx. 3" × 6" (7.5 × 15cm)
2 pieces of plywood 3" × 4" (7.5 × 10cm)
tape
glue
nails
hammer
2 U-shaped brads or paper clips
cork
U-shaped magnet
plastic knitting needle
6-volt battery
covered copper wire

What to do:
Use a hammer and a sharp nail to punch a hole approximately an inch (2½cm) from the top of each of the smaller pieces of wood. Make sure the knitting needle moves freely in the plywood holes. Then nail or glue one of the smaller pieces to each side of the larger piece of wood, as in illustration A. Push in two brads or tape on opened clips in the center of the base.

Choose a cork that is small enough to fit easily between the poles of your magnet.

Cut off two 4-inch (10 cm) strips of wire to serve as lead-in wires. Scrape the ends. Leaving an inch or two free at each end, wind the rest of the wire around the cork 30 or 40 times. Then scrape the insulation from the two free ends of the coiled wire.

Insert the needle through the first plywood hole, through the cork and then through the second plywood hole. Secure it with a small lump of clay or tape. See illustration B.

B

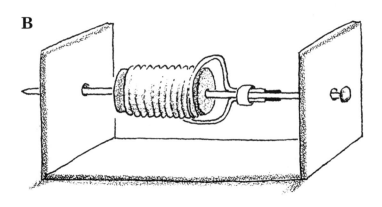

Tape the coiled wire to opposite sides of the knitting needle just above the bared ends.

Connect one end of the lead-in wires to the posts of the battery. Thread the two lead-in wires through the brads (or clips) and then stretch them up so that they make contact with the bared ends of the wire coil. See illustration C.

C

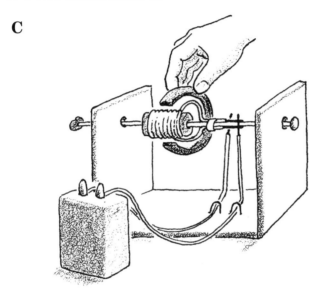

Finally, hold the magnet around the coil so that it can turn without touching the magnet. Start the motor by moving the cork with your finger.

What happens:
As long as you hold the magnet around the coil, the motor will move by itself.

Why:
The magnet converts electrical energy into mechanical energy. It causes the wire that carries the current to move, along with anything attached to it.

Charged!

You can demonstrate what goes on in a watch.

You need:
two pieces of wire
a battery
a small compass (or a needle, a magnet, a thin
  cork, a dish)

What to do:
If you don't have a compass, you can make one by
magnetizing a needle. Stroke it about 50 times in
one direction with either pole of a magnet. Then
float a cork in a dish of water and carefully center
the needle on it. Attach the wires to the two battery
terminals and make contact with the compass.

What happens:
The compass needle moves.

Why:
When electrons flow through a wire they produce a
magnetic field around the wire. This changes electrical energy into mechanical energy. The coil in a
watch concentrates this magnetic field and so enables
it to convert electric energy into mechanical energy.

Coin Battery

You can make a small battery of your own. Just empty your pockets of your coins.

You need:

vinegar or lemon juice
19 1" × 1" (2.5 × 2.5cm)
   strips of paper toweling

10 copper coins
10 metal coins—any
   metal except copper

What to do:

Soak the paper strips in the vinegar or lemon juice. Make a pile of the coins, alternating copper and the other metal. Separate each kind with one of the vinegar or lemon-soaked paper strips. Moisten one fingertip on each hand and hold the pile of coins between those fingers.

What happens:

You get a slight electric shock.

Why:

The vinegar or lemon, an acid solution, conducts the electricity created by the separated different metals of the two coins. It is a wet cell, a kind of battery.

A battery is usually made up of two metals (a zinc container and a carbon rod) separated by blotting paper soaked in a strong acid. A chemical reaction between the two metals produces a current of electrons between the two poles, and the chemical energy is converted into electrical energy. The battery is a storehouse of energy that wears out when the chemicals it contains are used up.

QUARTZ CRYSTAL CLOCKS

The invention of Dr. Warren A. Marrison, the quartz crystal clock dates back to 1929. Electric current makes the quartz vibrate like a violin string, at a number of frequencies depending on its thickness and the electrical power applied. This is called the piezoelectric effect.

In contrast to the balance wheel, which swings back and forth a few times a second, the crystal molecules swing back and forth at least 32,768 times a second, turning the electric current off and on each time. In an area of less than a half inch (one centimeter), the modern quartz crystal watch has a crystal the size of a match head, a tiny battery the size of a fingernail, and a microchip, which is an integrated circuit containing hundreds of thousands of transistors and resistors that conduct and control the amount of current flowing through.

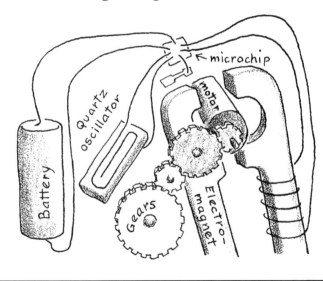

The Piezoelectric Effect

A simple cigarette lighter can demonstrate the effect of pressure on quartz.

You need:
a cigarette lighter

What to do:
Apply force with your thumb to the starter.

What happens:
You get a spark.

Why:
Inside the lighter is a wafer of quartz. When you apply pressure to it, you create electricity. In your watch, it is just the opposite. When electric current flows through, the wafer of quartz moves. Both of these changes in a crystalline substance such as quartz—creating electricity from pressure and creating movement from electricity— demonstrate the piezoelectric effect. *Piezo* comes from a Greek word meaning *to press* or *to squeeze.*

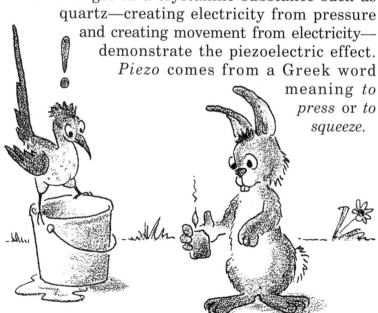

Digital Clocks

At first quartz clocks had dials and hands, but these often were replaced by digital "readouts" of hours and minutes and even sometimes seconds.

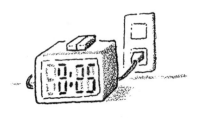

These numbers were formed by small luminous elements controlled by electrical signals.

There are different kinds of readouts. Some are LEDs (Light Emitting Diodes). When electric current runs through these electronic devices, it gives off a bright glow, either red, yellow, or green, depending on the material used. Readouts in small timepieces are generally LCD (Liquid Crystal Display). The creamy gray liquid crystals block the passage of light and thus turn black when current is applied. The result is a black digit on a gray background. Both result in squared-off digits formed from 7-section rectangles, parts of which light up and parts of which stay dark.

You need:
pencil and paper
eraser

What to do:
Copy the following form, made up of 7 straight lines forming a rectangle. Then blacken the sections of the form that make the number you want.

For instance, if you want to

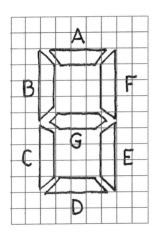

create a 6, blacken all the lines except F, the upper right one, and A, the top one. Then erase (or lighten) F and A. If you need to create a 5, blacken all the lines except F and C. For a 1, blacken only B and C and erase the others.

What happens:
You can make all of the numbers by selecting which lines to highlight and which to eliminate. Digital clocks are coded to do this electrically.

Why:
Perhaps you understand now why the shape of numbers and letters in digital readouts take some getting used to. They certainly don't resemble printed or cursive writing. The vibrations back and forth of the flake of quartz are counted by a binary logic gate, a kind of switch. Every time the count reaches the number of vibrations that a particular crystal makes in a second, the switch sends a pulse to the display unit and the watch records the passage of another second. Other switches on the same chip count 60 seconds and update the minute display; others count minutes to update the hour.

Glowing in the Dark

Early on, clocks and watches were made with chimes to give the time after dark. But during World War I, when a chiming watch might have given away the wearer's position to the enemy, watch-makers developed a watch that glowed in the dark. Hands and dials were painted with radium. When radium was found to be a hazardous substance, particularly to the workers who painted with it, less dangerous materials were used.

Available now are sports watches with phosphorescent hands that glow because the phosphorus coating converts the energy of sunlight into electronic vibrations and releases it in the form of light.

Also marketed are battery-operated watches with "Indiglo night lights." The watch face is coated with zinc sulfide diluted by a small amount of copper. When you press a button, electrical energy from the battery is converted by a microchip to a higher voltage, exciting electrons in the dial material which then provide a greenish light.

Timing the Past:
The Radioactive Clock

Scientists tell time backward by a radioactive clock that ticks away in ancient bones, in the wood of an ancient barge, and in all other material that has ever lived in the past 50,000 years. This radioactive clock is a slowly disintegrating form of the carbon atom called carbon 14. Plants obtain carbon dioxide from the atmosphere and animals eat the plants. After the animals and plants die, radioactive decay begins. The rate of radioactive decay is measured in terms of half-life, the time required for half of an element to decay. A once-living organism loses half of its carbon 14 in about 5,000 years, half of what's left in the next 5,000, and half of that for the third 5,000. Nothing detectable remains after about 50,000 years. To determine the age of something that once lived—from cloth to seashells—scientists figure out its carbon-14 content and compare it with the content of a modern sample.

Radioactive atoms in earth, air and water have also provided "clocks" by which the ages of rocks and fossils older than 50,000 years can be measured. Like that of carbon 14, the rate of radioactive decay is measured in terms of half-life. In one half-life, half of the original atoms decay; in a second half-life, half of that remains, and so on.

Measurements of the decay of uranium, for instance, give it a half-life of about 4.5 billion years.

Atomic Clocks

An atomic clock is based on the action of the electrons in an atom, which vibrates naturally and whose frequency is immune to the temperature and friction problems that plague mechanical clocks.

In 1967 the General Assembly on Weights and Measurements changed the definition of a second to the frequency with which the atom of the metal cesium vibrates back and forth—9,192,631,770 times a second. The more vibrations a timekeeper makes in one second, the more accurate it is. Atomic timetellers are accurate to one billionth of a second in 24 hours.

The first molecular clock, which used ammonia gas, was built in 1949 by H. Lyons at the United States National Bureau of` Standards. In 1955 L. Essen and J. V. L. Parry built the first cesium atomic clock at the National Physical Laboratory in England.

You can see this latest method of keeping time at the laboratories of the National Bureau of Standards in Boulder, Colorado. It looks like no clock you have ever seen—more like a sewer pipe—a stainless steel pipe 20' (6m) long with a 16-inch diameter (40cm), which is actually a cesium-beam tube. Cesium is a soft silvery metal that looks a little like mercury.

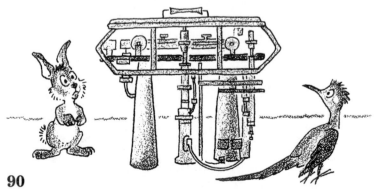

Time Machines—and More

A few scientists have been investigating claims that some people have actually gone back in time, that time can go backward. They are also looking into the possibility that some people see into the future. They debate whether dreams are sometimes a form of insight into what is going to happen, a form of "future time." Some philosophers through the years have suggested that time is a circle, doubling back on itself.

While it's easy to define the measuring of time, time itself is more difficult to describe. Some have questioned whether time exists at all. Everyone—from the physicist to the psychologist to the philosopher—has a different explanation. Einstein's theories—proved in laboratory atomic experiments—challenge some of our most basic beliefs about time. They indicate time slows down at speeds approaching the speed of light.

It takes light from the Sun about eight minutes and light from Pluto about five hours to reach Earth. But light from the nearest star—other than the Sun—we now see twinkling in the sky actually has been traveling at the speed of light for more than four years. And some of the more distant stars' light has been traveling at that speed for more than two million years by the time astronomers see it on their telescopes.

With space exploration and the possibility of life on other planets, what more will the future teach us about the past—and the future?

GLOSSARY

Balance spring—the hairspring, a long, fine, spiral spring that determines the time of the swing of the balance.

Constellation—a cluster of stars that make up a pattern. Ancient peoples saw these as pictures, giving them names like Big Bear, Leo the Lion, Orion the Hunter, etc.

Diode—an electronic device that has two terminals and converts alternating current to direct current.

Earth's Axis—an imaginary line from the North to South Pole. It takes a day for the Earth to make a complete turn on its axis.

Equinox—the days when the Sun is directly above the equator and day and night are of equal length. March 21 is called the vernal equinox, September 21 is the autumnal equinox.

Escapement—a device that regulates the speed of the train of gear wheels of a clock or watch. It usually consists of a wheel with teeth and an anchor that releases one tooth on the heel at a given interval.

Frequency—the number of complete cycles or swings per second.

Gears—toothed wheels that intermesh so that one wheel turns to drive the other. A screw (a worm) or a toothed shaft (a rack) may replace one of the wheels.

Hertz (HZ)—a unit of frequency equal to one cycle per second, named for physicist Heinrich Hertz.

Horologists—clock-makers.

L.A.T.—local apparent time, which is time measured by the actual movement of Earth and the Sun and differs from season to season and from place to place. It is the time measured by the sundial.

Latitude—the distance in degrees of a point on Earth from the equator.

LCD (liquid crystal display)—an alphanumeric display on digital watches and calculators made up of a liquid sandwiched between layers of glass or plastic. It becomes opaque when an electric current is passed through it. The contrast between the opaque and transparent areas forms visible characters.

LED (light emitting diode)—a semi-conductor electron tube that converts electric power (applied voltage) to light and is used in digital displays, as a digital watch or a calculator.

L.M.T.—local mean time, which measures the average speed at which the Moon moves in its ellipse and Earth spins in its orbit. Our clocks and watches show local mean time.

Longitude—the distance east or west on Earth's surface, measured in degrees up to 180°, or the difference in time between the meridian passing through a particular place and the prime meridian at Greenwich, England.

Megahertz (MHZ)—one million cycles per second.

Meridians—imaginary lines running along Earth's surface from the North to the South Pole.

Oscillator—an instrument that produces a steady rhythm of swings or vibrations.

Piezoelectric effect—electricity created by pressure or pressure created by electricity, especially in a crystal like quartz.

Planetarium—an optical device for projecting astronomical images; a model or representation of the solar system.

Summer solstice—longest day because the tilt of Earth lets the Sun shine longest (June 21 in the Northern Hemisphere, December 21 in the Southern Hemisphere).

Winter solstice—the day when Earth is tilted farthest away from the Sun, and so the day is the shortest (December 21st in the Northern Hemisphere, June 21 in the Southern Hemisphere).

ACKNOWLEDGMENTS

I would like to thank a number of people and organizations to whom I am indebted for their help during my exploration of time. The National Association of Watch and Clock Collectors and the American Clock and Watch Museum in Bristol, Conn., responded most graciously to my initial request for guidance. Clock collector Michael Glass generously shared his expertise and his clock books. Science teacher Sally Aberth looked over the section on water clocks.

Astrophysicist Neil de Grasse Tyson, Director of New York City's Hayden Planetarium, reviewed the chapter on star time. Lloyd Motz, Astronomy Professor Emeritus of Columbia University, made suggestions for that chapter and those on the moon and sundials.

Clock repairer Geoff Pommer of Ilana went over the sections on mechanical and electrical clocks and watches.

My special thanks to the New York Public Library's many cooperative librarians who searched far and wide for the books requested. Among those were helpful books by Irving Adler, Marilyn Burns, T.R. Reid, Gabriel Reuben, B.A. Rey, Albert Vaughn, Bernie Zubrowski, J.B. Priestley, and, of course, James Jesperson.

And, of course, many thanks to my conscientious editor, Sheila Barry.

INDEX

96